TinkerActive

EARLY SKILLS · WORKBOOKS

Ages 4+

Math

TINKER TOWN TREATS!

TOY SHOP

BARBER SHOP

HARD...

written by **Nathalie Le Du**

educational consulting by **Casey Federico**, MSEd

illustrated by **Gustavo Almeida**

odd dot

NEW YORK

T0016588

120 Broadway
New York, NY 10271
OddDot.com

ISBN: 978-1-250-78440-7

WRITER Nathalie Le Du

ILLUSTRATOR Gustavo Almeida

EDUCATIONAL CONSULTANT Casey Federico, MSEd

CHARACTER DESIGNER Anna-Maria Jung

DESIGNERS Abby Dening and Caitlyn Hunter

EDITOR Kate Avino

Our books may be purchased in bulk for promotional, educational, or business use. Please contact your local bookseller or the Macmillan Corporate and Premium Sales Department at (800) 221-7945 ext. 5442 or by email at MacmillanSpecialMarkets@macmillan.com.

DISCLAIMER
The publisher and author disclaim responsibility for any loss, injury, or damages caused as a result of any of the instructions described in this book.

TinkerActive is a trademark of Odd Dot.

Printed in China by Hung Hing Off-set Printing Co. Ltd., Heshan City, Guangdong Province

First edition, 2023

1 3 5 7 9 10 8 6 4 2

Meet the MotMots!

Amelia   Brian   Callie   Dimitri   Enid   Frank

Sorting and Patterns

Brian and Callie are heading to Main Street in Tinker Town.

Paste the sticker that **matches** each empty shape below.

★ HEY, GROWN-UPS! ★

You can find all the stickers at the end of this book. Peeling stickers is great practice for improving fine motor control. If your child has difficulty at first, peel one corner and ask them to remove the sticker the rest of the way. Your child will gradually develop the skills to peel and place stickers on their own!

Dimitri loves to smell the flowers. Circle the objects that are the **same color**. Then say the name of the color aloud.

Good job! You earned a sticker! Choose one from page 127 and place it on your poster.

GOOD JOB! STICKER

Watch out for Frank! Color the objects so they **match**. Then say the name of the color aloud.

Enid and Amelia are shopping on Main Street. Cross out the object that is **different**.

Circle the object that is a **different color**. Then say the name of the color aloud.

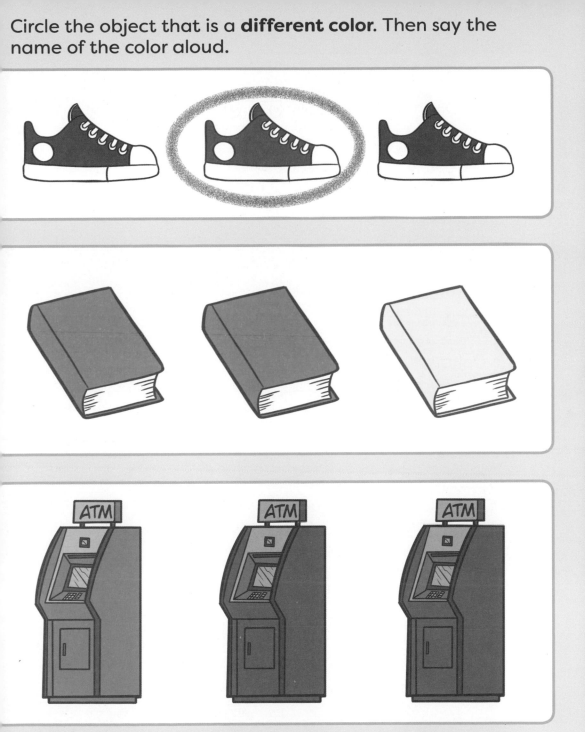

Callie spotted the ice cream truck! Color the objects so they are **different**. Then say the names of the colors aloud.

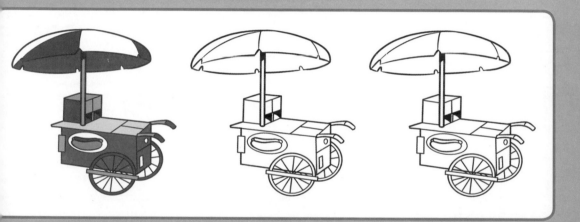

The MotMots are driving around Main Street.
With the help of an adult, cut along the ----------.
Then sort the cards by color. Next, shuffle the cards
and sort by vehicle type.

With the help of an adult, cut along the - - - - - - - - -.
Sort the cards by color, then by vehicle type.
Can you sort the objects in another way?

YOU DID IT!
STICKER

Look at the colors in each row and say the **pattern** aloud. Then copy the pattern below so the colors repeat in the same way.

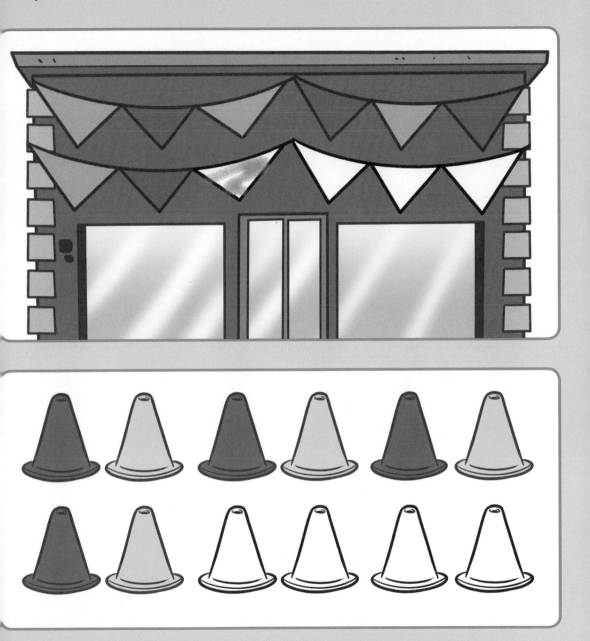

Look at the colors in each row and say the **pattern** aloud. Then color the missing fruit to fill in the pattern.

Look at the colors in each row and say the **pattern** aloud. Then color the missing flower to fill in the pattern.

11

Look at the colors in each row and say the **pattern** aloud.
Then draw and color more candy to **extend** the pattern.

Let's TINKER!

Gather these tools and materials.

Play with patterns! How are your materials the same or different? **Sort** them in different ways to find out, then make your own patterns. Or, **tear up** your colored construction paper and make your own patterns.

Scissors
(with an adult's help)

Construction paper
(5 or more colors)

Glue stick

Crayons

Optional: buttons, pom-poms, pipe cleaners, or any other decorative materials

Let's MAKE!

Flower Patterns!

1. With the help of an adult, **cut** a flower stem and leaves from construction paper.

2. **Glue** the stem and leaves onto a piece of paper.

3. **Choose** 2 colors of construction paper for your petals. With the help of an adult, **stack** the paper and cut 3 petal shapes to make 6 total petals.

4. **Arrange** your flower petals in a pattern and say the pattern aloud. Then **glue** each piece to the top of your flower stem.

Let's ENGINEER a solution!

Enid wanted to buy some flowers for Callie. But the florist didn't have any flowers with Callie's favorite petal pattern—red, orange, yellow, red, orange, yellow, and so on. How can Enid make Callie a flower with her favorite colors? **Create** a solution with your materials. What is your favorite pattern? **Make** a flower for yourself, too!

You're a TinkerActive CHAMPION!

You've earned an extra-special sticker. Peel it and place it anywhere you'd like on your poster.

Identifying and Ordering Numbers Up to 20

Dimitri and Frank are grocery shopping! Draw a line **from 1 to 10** while saying each number aloud.

★ HEY, GROWN-UPS! ★

Path-drawing and number-tracing activities include start and stop symbols to guide your child through the activity. Ask your child to trace the path with their finger first before moving on to a pencil.

Amelia is in a rush! Draw a line **from 1 to 10** while saying each number aloud.

Trace each number with your finger or a pencil, and say it aloud. Then count the fingers or objects aloud.

Trace each number with your finger or a pencil, and say it aloud. Then count the fingers or objects aloud.

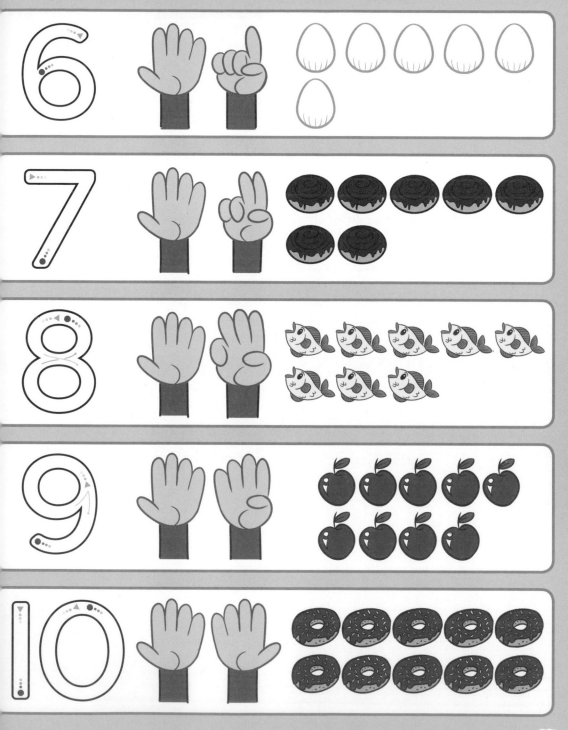

Draw a line **from 1 to 15** while saying each number aloud.

Trace each number with your finger or a pencil, and say it aloud. Then count the fruits or vegetables aloud.

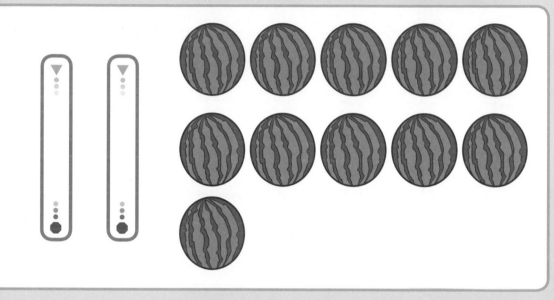

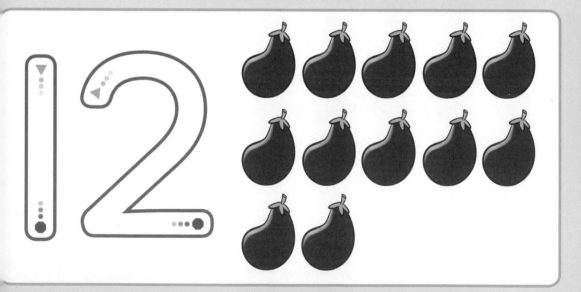

★ HEY, GROWN-UPS! ★

Often, children confidently count to 10, then become unsure of numbers 11 through 19, and then pick up steam again at 20. That's because numbers 11 through 19 are the only numbers that distort the counting pattern. To practice the teens, write and recite the numbers 1 through 20 on the write-and-wipe game board again and again!

Trace each number with your finger or a pencil, and say it aloud. Then count the fruits or vegetables aloud.

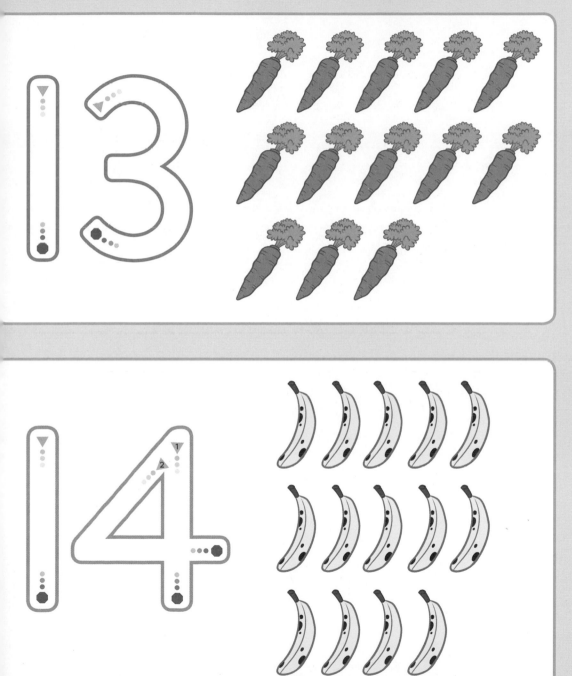

Trace each number with your finger or a pencil, and say it aloud. Then count the fruits or vegetables aloud.

 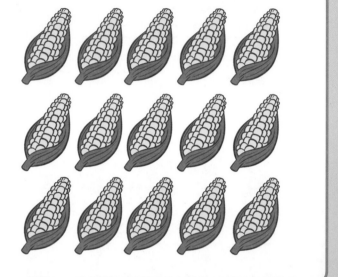

Color by number.

11	yellow	14	blue
12	orange	15	pink
13	purple		

★ HEY, GROWN-UPS! ★

This is a lot of coloring for a little learner to do! Recognize their hard work with a phrase like "This is a big project!" Encourage them to finish by saying something like "I love to see how hard you are working! Keep going!"

23

Draw a line **from 1 to 20** while saying each number aloud.

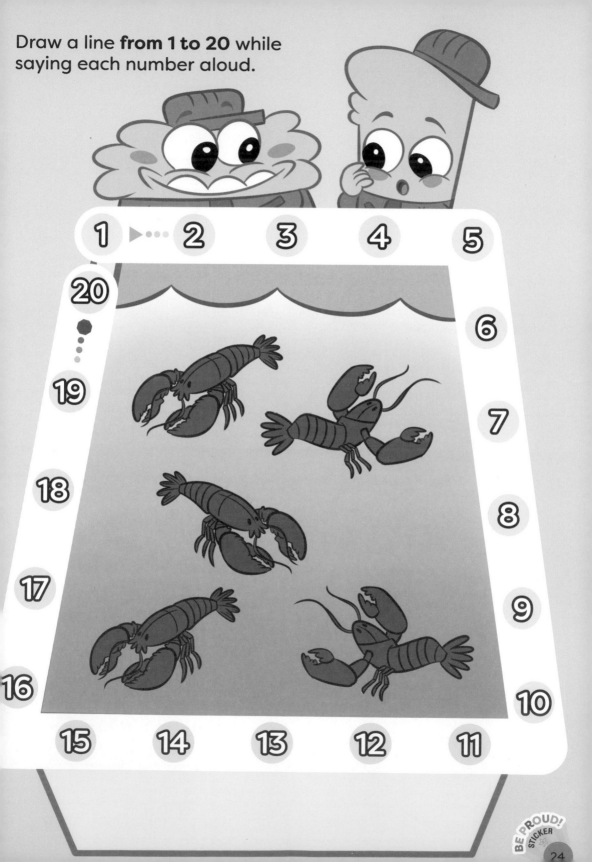

Draw a line **from 1 to 20** while saying each number aloud.

Trace each number with your finger or a pencil, and say it aloud. Then count the objects aloud.

Trace each number with your finger or a pencil, and say it aloud. Then count the objects aloud.

Color by number.

- **16** yellow
- **17** orange
- **18** red
- **19** green
- **20** purple

Gather these tools and materials.

Tinker with each object! How does each feel, taste, and sound? How much of each object do you have? Do you have 20 of any item? **Touch** each one as you count them aloud.

1½ cups rolled oats

½ cup nut or seed butter

⅓ cup chocolate chips

⅓ cup maple syrup or honey

Bowl and spoon

Aluminum foil

Cereal box or egg carton

Let's **MAKE!**

No-Bake Bites!

1. Add the oats, nut or seed butter, chocolate chips, and syrup or honey to a large bowl.

2. Mix together well.

●●●▶

29

3. **Cover** the bowl with aluminum foil and chill in the refrigerator for 30 minutes.

4. **Scoop** a spoonful of the mixture and roll it into a ball with your palms. **Repeat** with the remaining oat mixture. How many bites did you make? **Count** them, then enjoy!

Let's ENGINEER a solution!

The oven is broken in the bakery section, so Dimitri made No-Bake Bites! But Dimitri needs a box that can keep each ball separate. How can he store 20 bites without them sticking together? **Build** a container for your No-Bake Bites that will fit 20 balls so they don't touch.

You're a TinkerActive CHAMPION!

The MotMots are visiting the bookstore!
Count the  in each shelf aloud.
Then trace the number with your finger or a pencil.

Read the number and count the 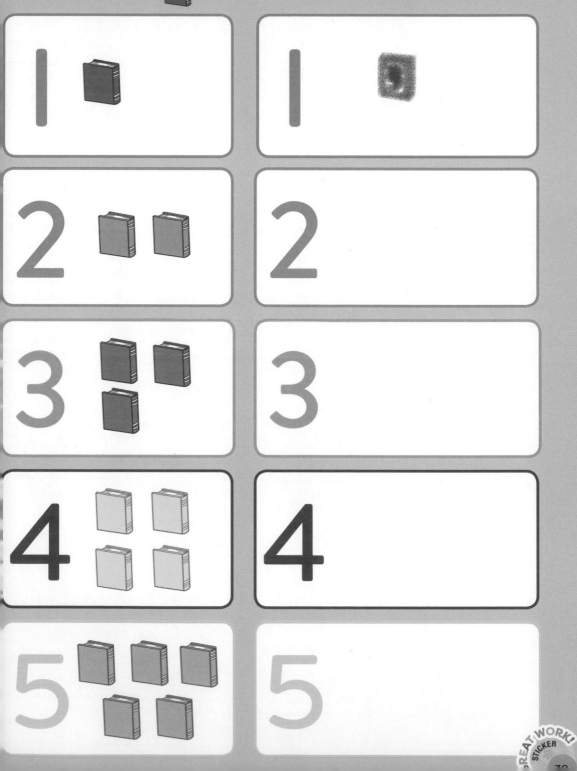. Then draw the same number of book.

Count the  aloud. Then trace the number with your finger or a pencil.

Read the number and count the 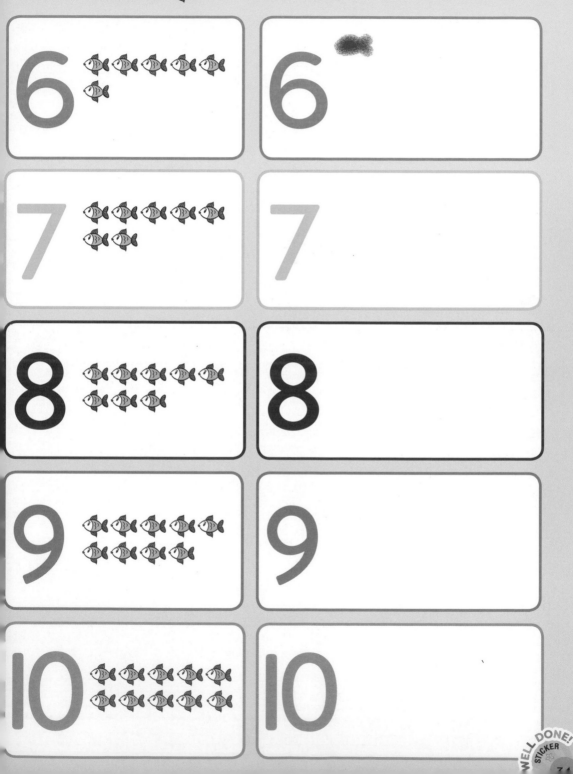. Then draw the
same number of fish.

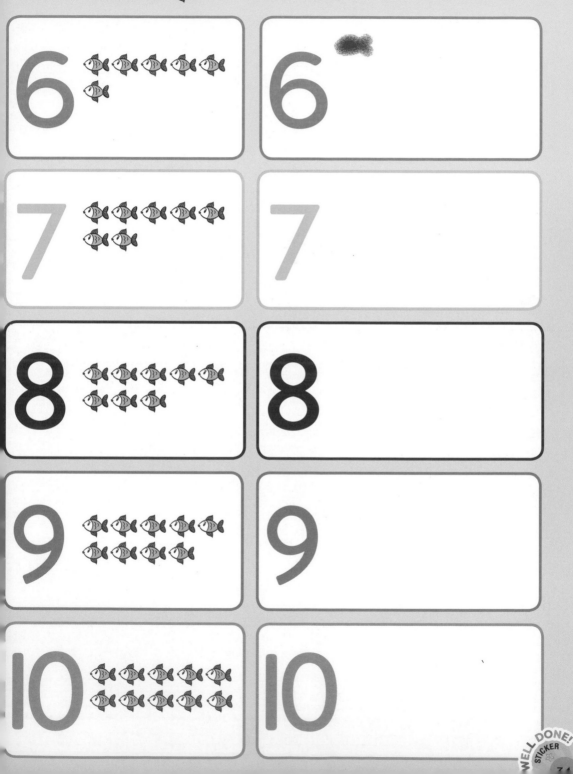

Color by number.

1 = green   4 = orange

2 = purple   5 = brown

3 = blue

★ HEY, GROWN-UPS! ★
As your child gains confidence with numbers, they will begin to subitize, which is to instantly know the amount of objects in a small set—rather than counting each object. So, for example, if you roll a 3 on a die, your child will immediately say, "3!" without counting the first, second, and third dots.

Color by number.

6 = green   9 = orange

7 = purple   10 = pink

8 = blue

Count the ⬜ in each row aloud. Then trace the number with your finger or a pencil.

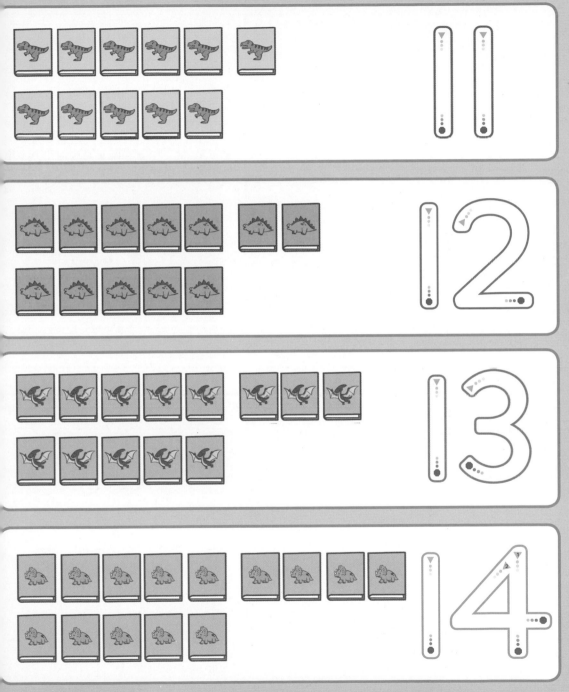

Read the number and count the 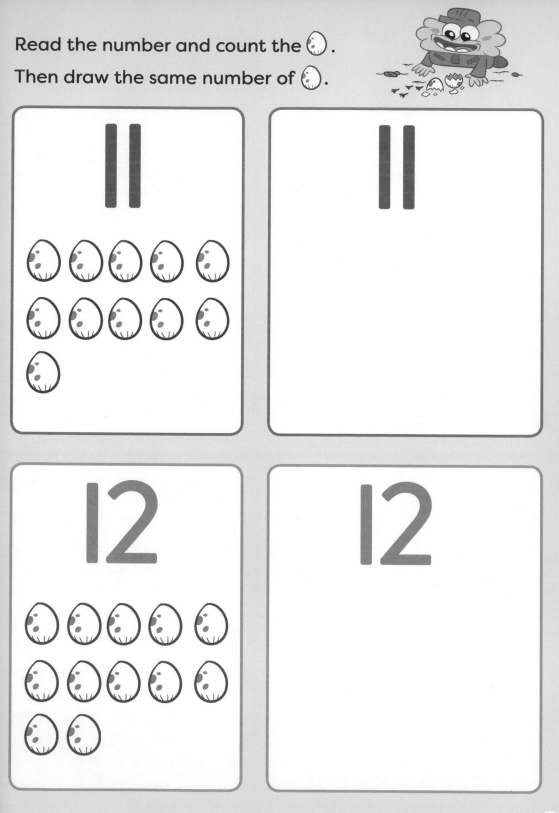 .

Then draw the same number of 🥚 .

11

11

12

12

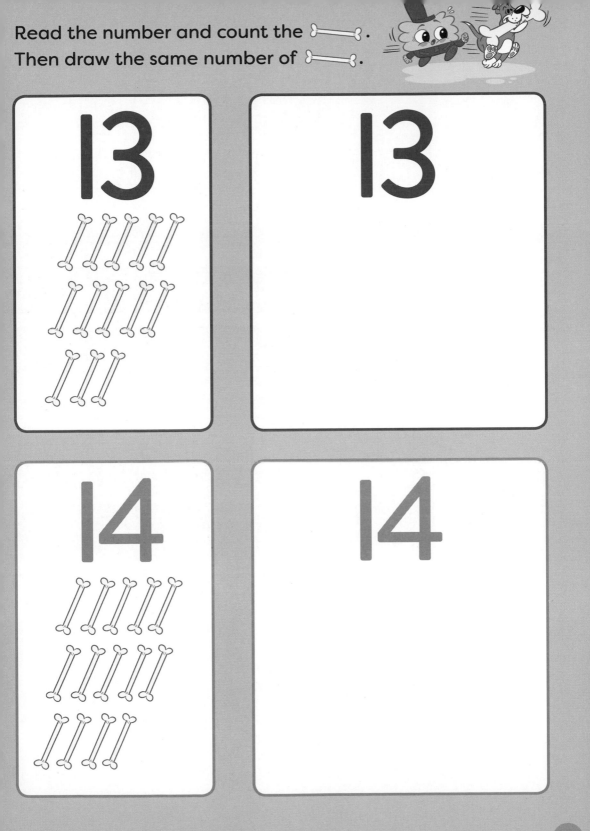
13

13

14

14

Count the 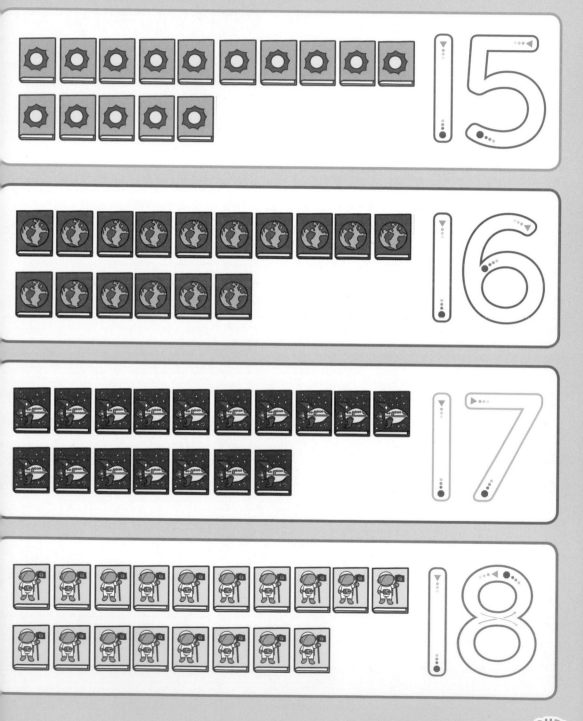 in each row aloud. Then trace the number with your finger or a pencil.

15

16

17

18

BE PROUD! STICKER

Read the number and count the .
Then draw the same number of .

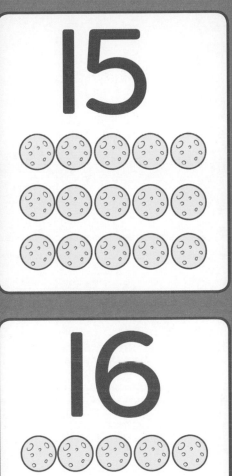

15

15

16

16

★ HEY, GROWN-UPS! ★

Is your child obsessed with rockets? Or dinosaurs? Or unicorns? Challenge them to draw 15 of their favorite things on the write-and-wipe game board and count aloud as they draw. Free drawing not only allows for creative expression, but it will also continue to build your child's hand strength and motor-control skills.

Read the number and count the .
Then draw the same number of .

17

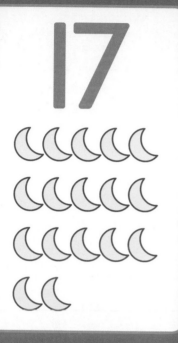

17

18

18

Count the  in each row aloud.

Then trace the number with your finger or a pencil.

Read the number and count the  .
Then draw the same number of ⚡ .

19

19

20

20

Gather these tools and materials.

Push and move your objects around. What makes each object different? Can you separate them into groups? **Count** them aloud as you separate the objects into groups. Does any group have 20 items?

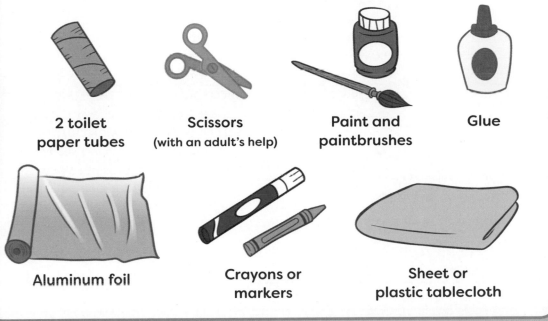

2 toilet paper tubes	**Scissors** (with an adult's help)	**Paint and paintbrushes**	**Glue**

Aluminum foil

Crayons or markers

Sheet or plastic tablecloth

Let's **MAKE!**

Superpower Counting Cuffs!

1. With the help of an adult, **cut** the toilet paper tubes lengthwise.

2. Paint your cuffs. Let dry.

3. Get the counting superpower stickers from page 128 and paste them onto the center of each cuff. Once you put on your cuffs, you can count *anything*!

Let's ENGINEER a solution!

Brian is the Counting Crusader, and his favorite number is 19. But he's missing a counting cap and cape to complete his costume. How can he make the rest of his costume and save the day? And how can he show off his favorite number on his costume? **Make** a cape and cap to complete your own costume and celebrate your favorite number!

You're a TinkerActive CHAMPION!

Callie and Amelia are headed to the town square! Draw a line **from 1 to 10** while saying each number aloud.

WELCOME TO TINKER TOWN SQUARE

CITY HALL

Trace the missing numbers on the number line with your finger or a pencil. Then read the number line aloud **from 1 to 10**.

Draw a line **from 10 to 1** while saying each number aloud.

Trace the missing numbers on the number line with your finger or a pencil. Then read the number line aloud **from 10 to 1.**

Draw a line **from 1 to 15** while saying each number aloud.

★ HEY, GROWN-UPS! ★

Stories, games, songs, and movements that involve numbers are great tools to reinforce counting skills. The next time you are outside, challenge your child to spot 15 birds. Or make up a silly story or a song about a child who had 15 pet birds! Having fun with numbers will encourage a love of math!

Trace the missing numbers on the number line with your finger or a pencil. Then read the number line aloud **from 5 to 15.**

WAY TO GO! STICKER

Draw a line **from 15 to 1** while saying each number aloud.

Trace the missing numbers on the number line with your finger or a pencil. Then read the number line aloud **from 15 to 5**.

12 11 10 9 8 13 14 7 15 6 5

Draw a line **from 1 to 20** while saying each number aloud.

★ HEY, GROWN-UPS! ★

Don't forget to look back at some of your child's earlier work. Have their understanding of numbers and their motor-control skills improved? Bravo! Find that they need some extra practice identifying or writing a certain number? Draw it on the write-and-wipe game board for your child to name and trace.

Amelia got one scoop of every flavor! Trace the missing numbers on the number line with your finger or a pencil. Then read the number line aloud **from 10 to 20.**

Draw a line **from 20 to 1** while saying each number aloud.

Trace the missing numbers on the number line with your finger or a pencil. Then read the number line aloud **from 20 to 10**.

Draw a line **from each starting number** ▶··· **to 10.**
Say each number aloud as you go.

★ **HEY, GROWN-UPS!** ★

At this point, your child likely counts from the number 1 and onward with confidence. "Counting on" from higher numbers or "counting back" from a number are new skills they must master. Praise your child for trying new things and learning!

Draw a line **from each starting number** ▶••• to 10.
Say each number aloud as you go.

Gather these tools and materials.

Play with your materials. **Take** them apart and put them together. Can you put them together in a new way? **Count out** your objects. Then **move** them around and count them again. Did you get the same number? Why do you think that is?

Scissors
(with an adult's help)

Poster board or cardboard

Duct tape

Construction paper

Glue

Optional: hole punch, ruler or measuring tape, and square-shaped object, such as tissue box, book, or plate

# Let's **MAKE!**

Colossal Counting-Up Die!

1. With the help of an adult, **cut** a large square from your poster board or cardboard. (You can simply eyeball a square, measure one, or place a square-shaped object onto the poster board and trace around it.)

2. **Place** your square on the remaining poster board and cut an identical panel. **Repeat** until you have 6 identical panels in total.

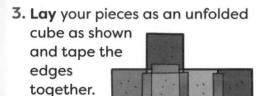

3. **Lay** your pieces as an unfolded cube as shown and tape the edges together.

4. **Fold** your cube together so the tape is inside the box, then tape the outside edges together.

5. **Cut** 21 circles out of your construction paper. **Count** them aloud. (Optional: Use a large hole punch to punch out circles. Use different colors for each number.)

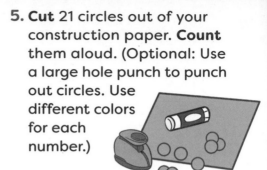

6. **Glue** the circles onto your die to make faces that show the quantities: 1, 2, 3, 4, 5, and 6.

7. **Roll** the die and count on from that number! How high can you count?

Let's **ENGINEER** a solution!

Frank's alligator, Chompy, is turning 20! For his birthday, Frank wants to make him a game to count down from 20. How can he make a game for his alligator's birthday?
Tinker with your die or make new dice altogether.
Try changing the rules to the Colossal Counting-Up game or make up a new game. The only goal is to count down from 20.

You're a TinkerActive CHAMPION!

Comparing Quantities

Enid is buying a present at the toy shop! Count the toys on each shelf. Then circle the shelves that have the **same** quantity.

Count the 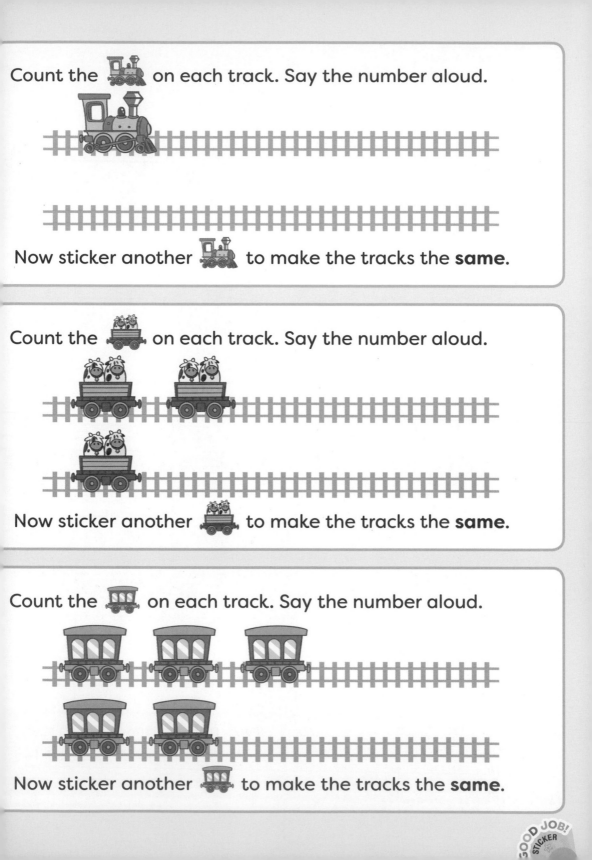 on each track. Say the number aloud.

Now sticker another to make the tracks the **same**.

Count the on each track. Say the number aloud.

Now sticker another to make the tracks the **same**.

Count the on each track. Say the number aloud.

Now sticker another to make the tracks the **same**.

GOOD JOB! STICKER

Count the toys on each shelf. Then circle the shelf that has **more** in each row.

Count the toys in each bin.
Say the number aloud.

Now draw toys in each bin
so there are **more**.

Count the toys on each shelf. Then circle the shelf that has **fewer** in each row.

Count the toys in each bucket.
Say the number aloud.

Now draw **fewer** toys in the
empty bucket in each row.

Count how many toys each MotMot has.
Say the number aloud.

Next, sticker **one more** toy. How many toys does each
MotMot have now? Say the number aloud.

Count how many fingers are showing on each hand. How many fingers are there in all? Say the number aloud and then trace the number.

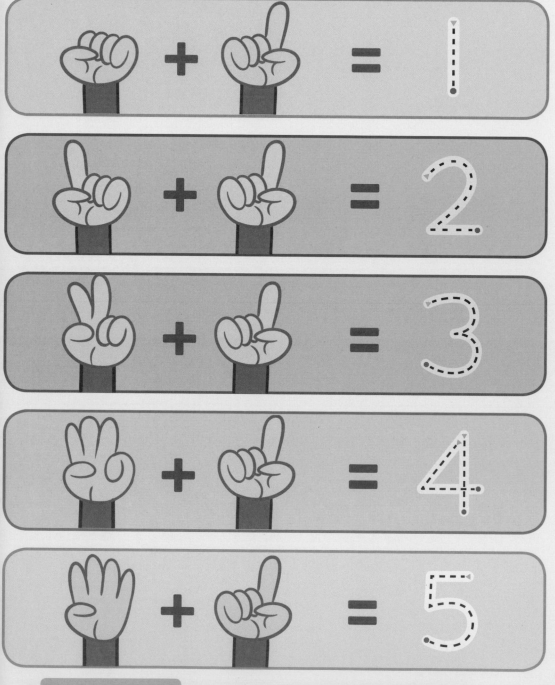

Count how many toys each MotMot has.
Say the number aloud.

Next, sticker **one more** toy. How many toys does each MotMot have now? Say the number aloud.

Count how many fingers are showing on each hand. How many fingers are there in all? Say the number aloud and then trace the number.

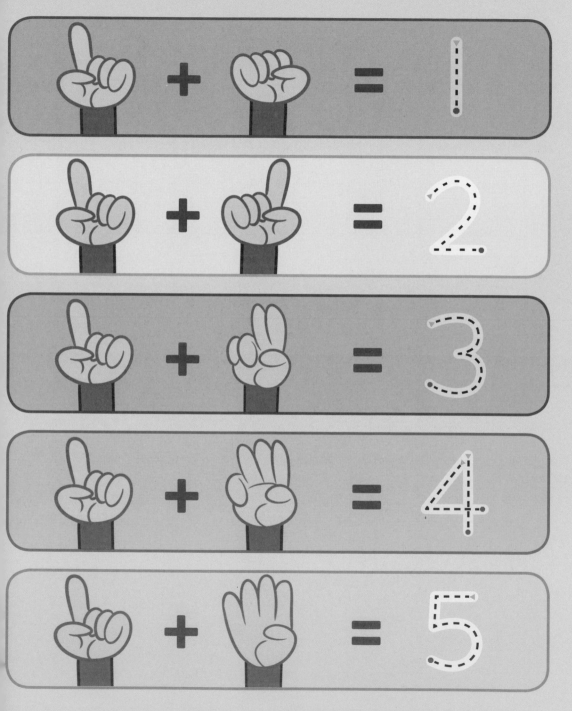

Count the white ◯ in each paint palette.
Say the number aloud.

Next, color **one** ◯ to add more paint to each palette.
How many white ◯ are left over? Say the number aloud.

Count the white 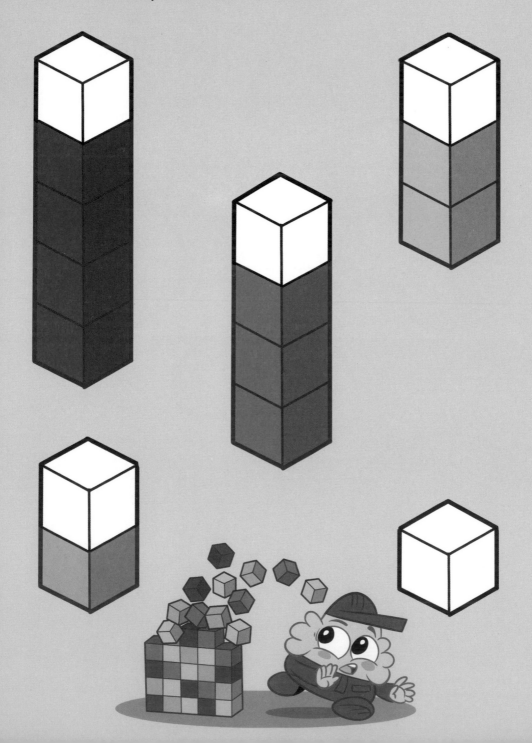 in each tower. Say the number aloud.
Next, color one 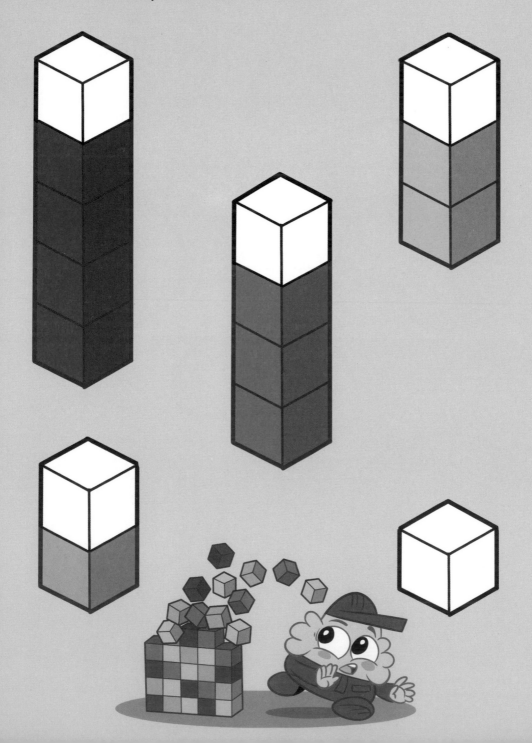 in each tower. How many white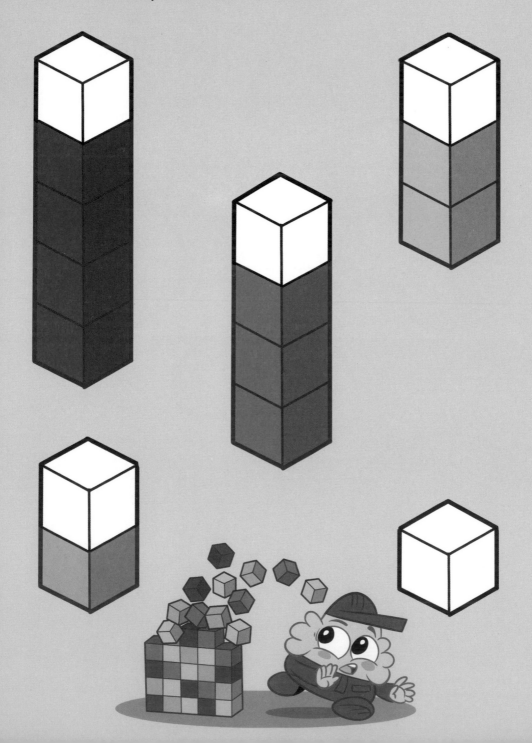
are left over? Say the number aloud.

Count the white 🎂 in each row. Say the number aloud.

Next, color one 🎂 in each row. How many white 🎂 are

left over? Say the number aloud.

★ HEY, GROWN-UPS! ★

Practice subtracting objects from a group (like eating one carrot from a bowlful) or practice subtracting parts from a whole (like a slice from a whole cake). Kids benefit when they are exposed to a wide range of problems—especially ones that reflect their day-to-day lives. And they'll have fun coming up with their own solutions as well!

Count how many fingers are showing on the first hand. Then count how many fingers are being put down on the next hand. How many fingers are left up? Say the number aloud and then trace the number.

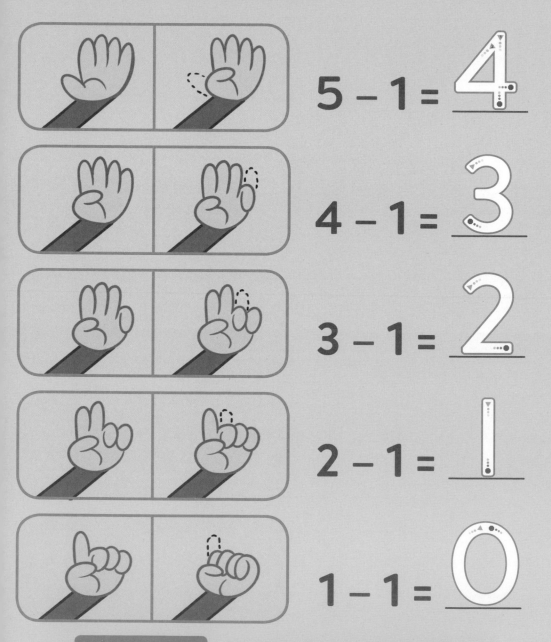

5 – 1 = 4

4 – 1 = 3

3 – 1 = 2

2 – 1 = 1

1 – 1 = 0

★ HEY, GROWN-UPS! ★

In addition to fingers, food is a great tool for practicing subtraction. The next time they have a snack like carrots or pretzel sticks, ask your child to count them aloud. Then tell them to eat one, and ask how many are left over. Continue the game until all the snacks are gone!

Let's TINKER!

Gather these tools and materials.

Explore your materials. Do any objects come apart? How many pieces make up the whole object?

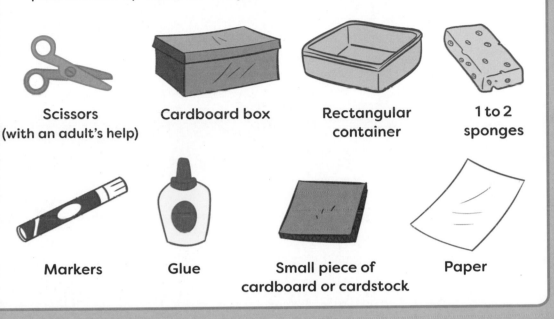

Scissors
(with an adult's help)

Cardboard box

Rectangular container

1 to 2 sponges

Markers

Glue

Small piece of cardboard or cardstock

Paper

Let's MAKE!

Cardboard Cash Register!

1. With the help of an adult, **cut** a hole in the bottom of your box that is slightly larger than your rectangular container. **Insert** the rectangular container to make a cash drawer.

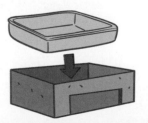

2. **Cut** your sponges to get 10 squares. Then **write** the numbers 0 through 9 on each square.

●●●▶

3. Glue your squares onto the lid of your shoebox.

4. Paste the CASH, CARD, and ENTER stickers from page 128 onto your cash register.

5. With the help of an adult, **cut** a slit in the top of your lid for "credit cards."

6. Paste the credit card sticker from page 128 onto a smaller piece of cardboard. With the help of an adult, **cut** the excess cardboard around it to make a credit card.

Let's ENGINEER a solution!

Amelia has a customer at her toy store! He wants to buy a doll that costs $1, but he only has a $5 bill. How many dollars should she give back and how can she make them?

You're a TinkerActive CHAMPION!

Brian needs new tools! Circle the tool that is **bigger** on each shelf. Cross out the tool that is **smaller** on each shelf.

Circle the object that is **bigger.**

Circle the object that is **smaller.**

Draw another 🔨 . Explain to an adult if it is bigger, smaller, or the same size.

With the help of an adult, cut out all the objects above and put them in order from smallest to largest, and then from largest to smallest.

Circle the tool that is **taller** in each box.
Underline the tool that is **shorter** in each box.

★ HEY, GROWN-UPS! ★

After learning to compare two items, children can develop the ability to compare three or more objects by size or by other attributes, such as by tallest to shortest or fastest to slowest.

Circle the object that is **taller**.

Circle the object that is **shorter**.

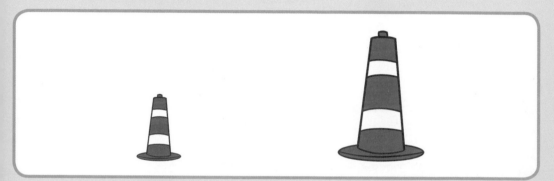

Draw another 🪣. Explain to an adult if it is taller, shorter, or the same height.

With the help of an adult, cut out all the objects above and put them in order from shortest to tallest and then from tallest to shortest.

Circle the tool that is **longer** on each worktable.
Underline the tool that is **shorter** on each worktable.

Circle the object that is **longer**.

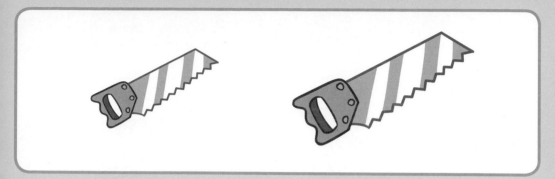

Circle the object that is **shorter**.

Draw another ▭. Explain to an adult if it is longer, shorter, or the same length.

With the help of an adult, cut out all the objects above and put them in order from shortest to longest and then from longest to shortest.

Circle the tools that are the **same size** in each row.
Underline the tool that is a **different size** in each row.

Circle the objects that are the **same size**.

Circle the object that is a **different size**.

Draw another . Explain to an adult if it is the same or a different size.

With the help of an adult, cut out all the objects above and put all the objects that are the same size together. Then order the remaining objects from smallest to largest and then from largest to smallest.

Circle the tools that are the **same length** in each box. Underline the tool that is a **different length** in each box.

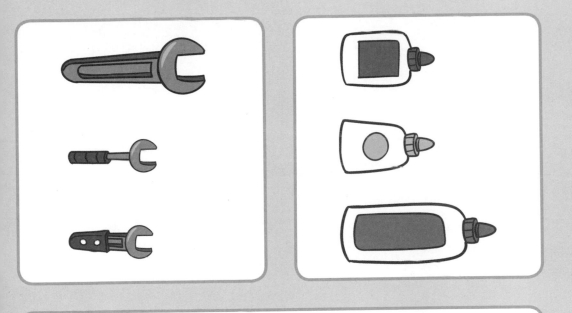

Circle the objects that are the **same length**.

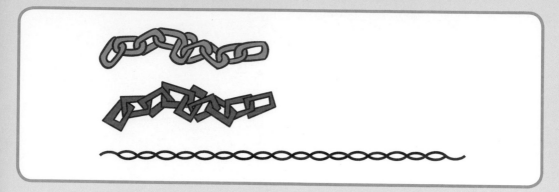

Circle the object that is a **different length**.

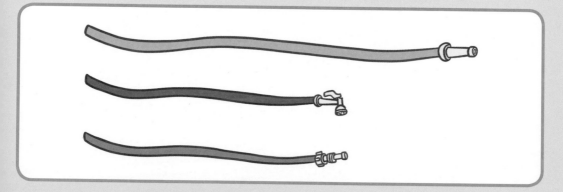

Draw another 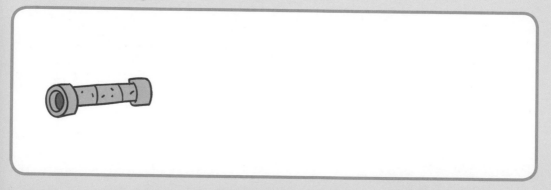. Explain to an adult if it is the same or a different length.

With the help of an adult, cut out all the objects above and put all the objects that are the same length together. Then, order the remaining objects from shortest to longest and then from longest to shortest.

How tall is each stack of blocks? Count aloud how many blocks are in each stack. Then trace the number.

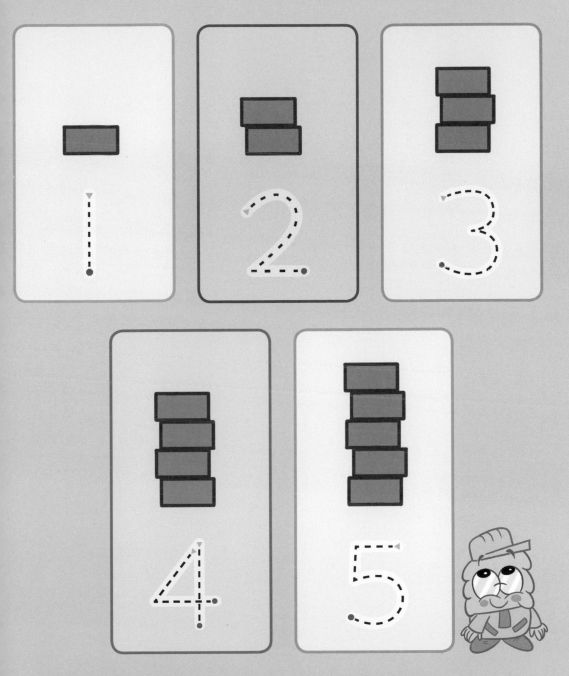

★ HEY, GROWN-UPS! ★

Using blocks, paper clips, or other objects that are familiar to kids is a great way to introduce units of measurement. Believe it or not, these are precursors for measuring with units like inches, pounds, and ounces. Find objects in your home that are the same size to have some hands-on measuring fun!

89

How tall is each stack of blocks? Count aloud how many blocks are in each stack. Then trace the number.

How long is each row of ?
Count aloud how many  are in each row. Then trace the number.

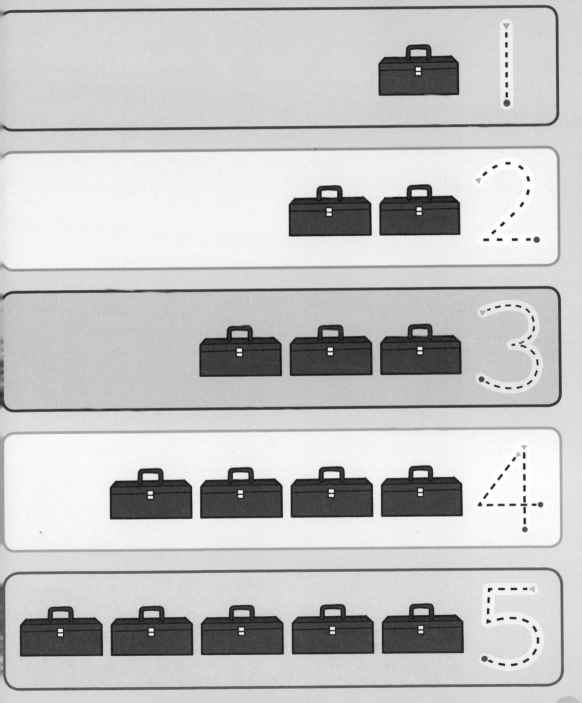

How long is each row of ? Count aloud how many are in each row. Then trace the number.

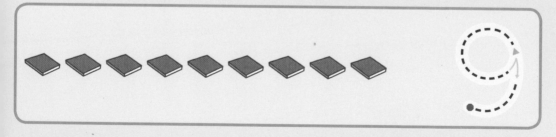

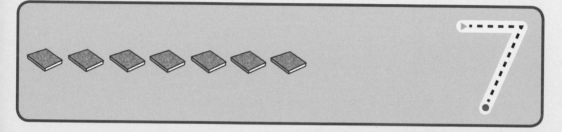

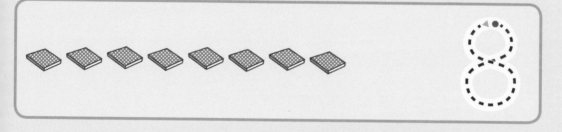

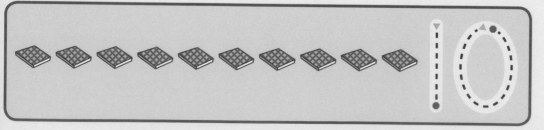

Let's **TINKER!**

Gather these tools and materials.

Arrange your tools and materials by size—smallest to largest. Then **arrange** them by length—longest to shortest. Did you have to move some objects? Why is that? Next, **try** height. What do you notice?

Shoebox

Pen

Cord or string

Paper cups

Gift wrap

Scissors
(with an adult's help)

Glue

Let's **MAKE!**

Shoebox Toolbox!

1. With the help of an adult, use your pen to **poke** two holes on each long side of the shoebox.

2. On one side of the shoebox, **thread** a piece of cord through both holes and knot the ends inside the shoebox. **Repeat** on the other side.

3. **Place** as many paper cups into your shoebox as needed so they fit snuggly.

4. **Pack** your toolbox with your favorite tools and materials!

Let's ENGINEER a solution!

Enid and Dimitri want to decorate their toolboxes with gift wrap. How can they figure out how much gift wrap they'll need to cover each toolbox completely? **Decorate** your toolbox lid using gift wrap, scissors, and glue. Can you cover it completely? How can you measure the paper to match the size of your lid?

You're a TinkerActive CHAMPION!

Spatial Reasoning: Location and Orientation

Frank needs food for his pet alligator, Chompy.

Sticker Frank's  **outside** the pet care center.

Sticker the 🐦 **inside** the store window.

PET CARE CENTER

OPEN

Draw another . Explain to an adult whether it is **inside** or **outside** the cave.

GOOD JOB! STICKER

Sticker the  **above** the bridge. Sticker the
below the bridge.

Draw another .
Explain to an adult
whether it is **above** or
below the cage.

WELL DONE!
STICKER

Sticker the  **on** the table.

Sticker the  **under** the table.

Draw another . Explain to an adult whether it is **on** or **under** the table.

Sticker the  **next to** the scratching post. Sticker the ⬤ **between** the cats.

Draw a  next to Enid.

Draw a cat between Dimitri and Frank.

With the help of an adult, cut along the ---------.

Arrange the pieces to reveal .

With the help of an adult, cut along the ----------.

Arrange the pieces to reveal _____ .

With the help of an adult, cut along the ----------.

Arrange the pieces to reveal  .

Let's TINKER!

Gather these tools and materials.

Explain to an adult where you found your tools and materials—*outside* your home, *inside* a cabinet, *under* your bed? **Arrange** your objects on a table and tinker with their locations. **Show** *outside* and *inside*, *above* and *below*, *on top of* and *under*, *next to* and *between*.

Scissors
(with the help
of an adult)

Cereal
box

Paint and paintbrushes
(blue and other colors)

Construction
paper

Glue

Found objects from *outside*,
such as rocks, grass, twigs,
shells, etc.

Stuffed animal

Let's MAKE!

Cereal Box Aquarium!

1. **Cut** a rectangular hole from the front of your cereal box.

2. **Paint** the *inside* of your box blue to create the "water."

●●● ▶

3. Paint the *outside* of your box in a different color.

4. With the help of an adult, **cut** fish out of the construction paper and decorate them however you'd like.

5. Glue your fish *onto* the water background.

6. Decorate your aquarium however you like—put rocks, grass, shells, and more *in* the bottom of the aquarium!

Let's ENGINEER a solution!

Callie's pet Great Dane, Boxer, keeps growing and growing. He needs a bigger home! How can she build a home for Boxer? **Pretend** your stuffed animal is Boxer. **Think about** how large it is, and what kind of home it might need— one that allows it to go *inside* and *outside* easily? What about a roof it can sit *under* when it rains? **Draw** a design on your write-and-wipe game board first, then build something that your stuffed animal can call home!

You're a TinkerActive CHAMPION!

Shapes and Patterns

Brian and Amelia found the sweets shop! Color the shapes that are the **same** in each row.

Color the shape that is **different** in each row.

GOOD JOB! STICKER

Trace the ☐ . Count the sides aloud as you trace.

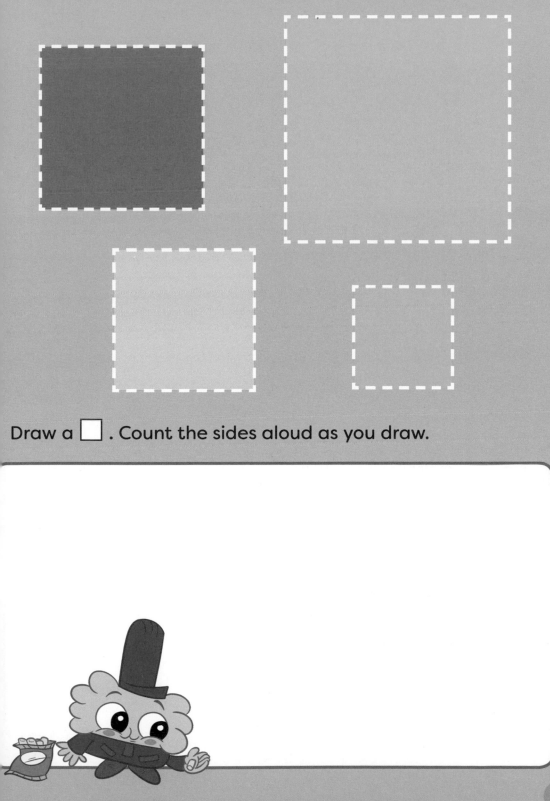

Draw a ☐ . Count the sides aloud as you draw.

113

Trace the △ . Count the sides aloud as you trace.

Draw a △ . Count the sides aloud as you draw.

WELL DONE! STICKER

Trace the ◯ . Does this shape have flat or round sides?
Say it aloud.

Draw a ◯ .

Trace the ☐ . Count the sides aloud as you trace.

Draw a ☐ . Count the sides aloud as you draw.

Trace the 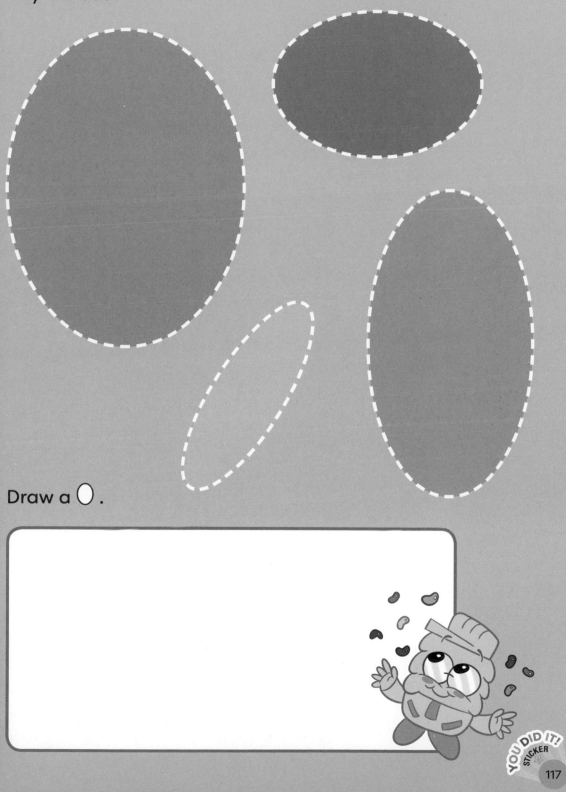 . Does this shape have flat or round sides?
Say it aloud.

Draw a ◯ .

YOU DID IT! STICKER

Trace the ◇ . Count the sides aloud as you trace.

Draw a ◇ . Count the sides aloud as you draw.

Brian and Frank are buying ice cream. Draw a line to **match** each shape at the top with a shape in the picture. Then say the name of each shape aloud.

Dimitri and Callie are baking cookies! Draw a line to **match** each shape at the top with a shape in the picture. Then say the name of each shape aloud.

BE PROUD!
STICKER

Draw a line to **match** each pair of shapes to their combined shape.

Draw a line to **match** each combined shape to their set of separate shapes.

★ **HEY, GROWN-UPS!** ★

Your child is learning that many shapes can be made up of or broken down into other shapes—this is the groundwork for more advanced math concepts like fractions and area. Encourage your child with phrases like "You matched all the shapes!" or "You are working hard to figure this out!"

Draw a line to **match** each set of shapes to their combined picture.

Peel the stickers from page 129 and paste them on this page to make new shapes or pictures. How can you combine them into your favorite shape?

Let's TINKER!

Gather these tools and materials.

Play with shapes! **Tear** or cut your construction paper into different shapes. **Experiment** with putting them together in new ways. What shapes can you create?

Crayons or markers

Construction paper

Scissors (with an adult's help)

Craft sticks

Optional: pipe cleaners, small pom-poms, dried beans, or rice

Shoebox or egg carton

Let's MAKE!   Shape Popsicles!

1. Draw a *rectangle* on a piece of construction paper.

2. Draw a *half circle* at one short end of your rectangle.

3. With the help of an adult, **cut** out your combined shape.

4. **Glue** a craft stick to your construction paper Popsicle. Let dry.

5. **Flip** over your Popsicle and decorate—draw toppings, cut up pipe cleaners for sprinkles, or use any other materials you have on hand.

6. **Repeat** steps 1 through 5 to make as many Popsicles as you like!

Let's ENGINEER a solution!

Frank made a new Popsicle flavor—MotMot Mango Mint! He wants to sell the Popsicles, but there's no place to stand them on the counter. How can he display his treats? **Design** a Popsicle holder for your Shape Popsicles. How could you stand them up?

You're a TinkerActive CHAMPION!

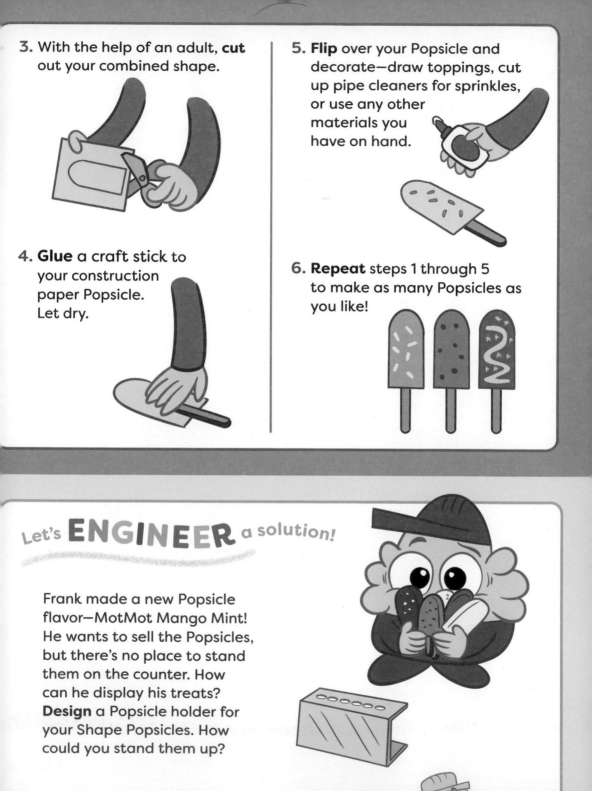